The Best Norwich City Football Chants Ever ...

The Best Norwich City Football Chants Ever …

The Best
Norwich City
Football Chants Ever ...

and also the rudest

A Fan

The Best Norwich City Football Chants Ever …

Unofficial and Unauthorised

All the chants in this book are common chants sung on the terrace during football matches, and are written here in a light hearted way they are not the thoughts and views of the authors.

Copyright © InterviewBooks.com
All rights reserved,
including the right of reproduction
in whole or in part in any form.

ISBN 978-0-557-19026-3

Designed and written by A Fan

The Best Norwich City Football Chants Ever ...

To all the Canaries fans out there, sing up for the lads!

The Best Norwich City Football Chants Ever ...

The Best Norwich City Football Chants Ever ...

Contents

Introduction 9

1. *Classic Chants* 11

2. *Norwich Heroes Songs* . . 19

3. *Give them some stick* . . . 27

4. *The referees a w*nker* . . 41

5. *The Best Norwich Websites* . . 45

6. *Norwich Supporters Clubs* . . 51

7. *The Best of the Rest* . . . 55

The Best Norwich City Football Chants Ever ...

Introduction

Thank you for taking the time to read "The Best Norwich City Football Chants Ever ...". In this book we take a light hearted look at the popular chants, sung from the terrace each week.

Most of the chants sung from the terrace are sung in a light hearted way but are sung to provoke the players or fans from the other team.

This book covers all of the popular songs; no chant has been kept out of this book for being politically incorrect or too rude.

Get ready to have a laugh at the other teams' expense ...

The Best Norwich City Football Chants Ever ...

Chapter 1

Classic Chants

The Best Norwich City Football Chants Ever ...

Chapter 1 - Classic Chants

And it's Norwich City
Norwich City F.C.
We're by far the greatest team
The world has ever seen

Kick off, throw it in, have a little scrimmage
Keep it low, a splendid rush, bravo, win or die
On the ball, City, never mind the danger
Steady on, now's your chance
Hurrah! We've scored a goal

Oh when the Canaries
(Oh when the Canaries)
Go marching in
(Go marching in)
Oh when the Canaries go marching in
I want to be in that number
When the Canaries go marching in

The Best Norwich City Football Chants Ever ...

Yellow Army
Yellow Army
Yellow Army
Yellow Army

We are Norwich
We are Norwich
We are Norwich
We are Norwich
We are Norwich

We love you Norwich
We do
We love you Norwich
We do
We love you Norwich
We do
Oh Norwich we love you

The Best Norwich City Football Chants Ever ...

E I, E I, E I, O
Up the league we go
When we win promotion
This is what we'll sing

We are Norwich
We are Norwich
Lambert is our king

Norwich till I die
I'm Norwich till I die
I know I am
I'm sure I am
I'm Norwich till I die

Come on Norwich
Come on Norwich
Come on Norwich
Come on Norwich

The Best Norwich City Football Chants Ever ...

(clap, clap, clap, clap, clap, clap clap)
Norwich
(clap, clap, clap, clap, clap, clap clap)
Norwich
(clap, clap, clap, clap, clap, clap clap)
Norwich

Come on you Yellows
Come on you Yellows
Come on you Yellows
Come on you Yellows

Stand up if your one nil up
Stand up if your one nil up
Stand up if your one nil up
Stand up if your one nil up

Hello, Hello. We are the City Boys
Hello, Hello. We are the City Boys
And if you are a Ipswich fan
Surrender or you die
We all follow the City

The Best Norwich City Football Chants Ever ...

Yarmy
Yarmy
Yarmy
Yarmy

Flying high up in the sky
We'll keep the green flag flying high
Flying high up in the sky
We'll keep the green flag flying high

We're the Barclay
We're the Barclay
We're the Barclay over here

We're the Snake Pit
We're the Snake Pit
We're the Snake Pit over here

Keep St George in my heart keep me English

Keep St George in my heart I pray

Keep St George in my heart keep me English

Keep me English till my dying day

The Best Norwich City Football Chants Ever ...

Follow, follow, follow
Follow the boys in yellow
We're the yellow and green
The world's best team
And it's off to the Premier we go

If you're standing
On a corner
With a blue scarf
Round your neck
Norwich boys
Will come and get ya
And we'll break
Your f*cking neck
La la la la

We are Norwich
We are Norwich
Super Norwich
We are Norwich
From the Light

Chapter 2

Norwich City Heroes Songs

The Best Norwich City Football Chants Ever ...

Chapter 2 - *Norwich City Heroes Songs*

Anthony McNamee
He looks F*ckin quick to me
With a Nick Nack paddy wack Give a dog a bone
Get Capello on the phone

Super, Super, Chris
Super, Super, Chris
Super, Super, Chris
Super, Chrissy Martin

Cody McDonald had a farm
E I E I O
And on that farm he scored a goal
E I E I O
With a goal scored here and a goal scored there
Left foot, right foot
Score em with either foot
Cody McDonald scored a goal
E I E I O

The Best Norwich City Football Chants Ever ...

Here we go, here we go, here we go
Youssef is better than Juninho
Say woah woah
Moroccan all over the world

Here we go, here we go, here we go
Youssef is better than Ronaldinhio
Say woah woah
Moroccan all over the world
(Tune: Rocking all over the world)

Oh Jamie, Jamie
Jamie, Jamie, Jamie, Jamie Cureton
Oh Jamie, Jamie
Jamie, Jamie, Jamie, Jamie Cureton
Oh Jamie, Jamie
Jamie, Jamie, Cureton

We F**kin Love Grant Holt
We F**kin Love Grant Holt
We F**kin Love Grant Holt
Grant Holt

The Best Norwich City Football Chants Ever ...

Na, na, na, na
Wesley Hoolahan
Hoolahan
Wesley Hoolahan

Paul Lambert's green army
NCFC
Paul Lambert's green army
NCFC
Paul Lamberts green army
NCFC

There's only one Paul Lambert
One Paul Lambert
He beat us 7-1 so they fired the Gunn
walking in a Lambert wonderland

One ginger Pele
There's only one ginger Pele
One ginger Pele
There's only one ginger Pele

The Best Norwich City Football Chants Ever ...

We love you Paul McVeigh
And if it's quite alright
We love you Paul McVeigh
Despite your lack of height
We love you Paul McVeigh
When you cross the ball
And we score

(Tune: I love you baby)

Matty Patersons Havin' A Party
Bring The Vodka And Bacardi

Alan Lee is one of us
One of us
One of us
Alan Lee is one of us
He hates Ipswich

McDonald
McDonald
he gets the ball and he scores a goal
McDonald
McDonald
He gets the ball and he scores a goal

The Best Norwich City Football Chants Ever ...

Brian Gunn
Brian Gunn
Brian, Brian Gunn
He's got no hair
But we don't care
Brian, Brian Gunn

The Best Norwich City Football Chants Ever ...

Chapter 3

Give them some stick

The Best Norwich City Football Chants Ever ...

Chapter 3   -   *Give them some stick*

You're not singing
You're not singing
You're not singing anymore
You're not singing anymore

Can you hear Ipswich sing? No, no

Can you hear Ipswich sing? No, no

Can you hear Ipswich sing

I can't hear a f*cking thing

Woah woah woah

If you all hate Ipswich clap your hands
If you all hate Ipswich clap your hands
If you all hate Ipswich
If you all hate Ipswich
If you all hate Ipswich clap your hands

The Best Norwich City Football Chants Ever ...

When I was just a little boy
I asked my mother what should I be
Should I be Norwich or should I be Ipswich
Here's what she said to me
Wash your mouth out son
And fetch your fathers gun
And shoot the Ipswich scum
And shoot the Ipswich scum
We hate Ipswich, we hate Ipswich

Always sh*t on the old blue and white
Da da, da da, de da de da de da
Always sh*t on the old blue and white
Da da, da da, de da de da de da

We forgot that
We forgot that
We forgot that you were here
We forgot that you were here

Sh*t ground no fans
Sh*t ground no fans
Sh*t ground no fans

The Best Norwich City Football Chants Ever ...

Oh Portman Road is full of sh*t
Oh Portman Road is full of sh*t
It's full of sh*t, sh*t and more sh*t
Oh Portman Road is full of sh*t

You're just small town Suffolk
Small town Suffolk
You're just small town Suffolk

In a town
Where I was born
Lived a team that we adored
But theirs a team that's f*cking sh*te
And they play in blue and white

Singing
Ipswich going down like a Russian submarine
A Russian submarine
A Russian submarine
Ipswich going down like a Russian submarine
A Russian submarine
A Russian submarine

The Best Norwich City Football Chants Ever ...

You're supposed to
You're supposed to
You're supposed to be at home
You're supposed to be at home

The wheels on your house go round and round
Round and round
Round and round
The wheels on your house go round and round
All day long

Sit down, shut up
Sit down, shut up
Sit down, shut up
Sit down, shut up
Sit down, shut up
Sit down, shut up

Away in a manger
No crib for his bed
The little Lord Jesus laid down and he said:

We hate Ipswich

We hate Ipswich

The Best Norwich City Football Chants Ever ...

Premiership
Your having a laugh
Premiership
Your having a laugh
Premiership
Your having a laugh
Premiership
Your having a laugh
Premiership
Your having a laugh

Shall we sing a
Shall we sing a
Shall we sing a song for you
Shall we sing a song for you

We had joy
We had fun
We had Ipswich on the run
But the fun didn't last coz the f*ckers ran to fast

The Best Norwich City Football Chants Ever ...

Hark now hear
The City Sing
Ipswich ran away
And we will fight for ever more
Because of Derby Day

You are a farmer
A dirty farmer
Your only happy when making hay
Your mums an info
Your dads a scarecrow
So please don't take my tractor away

Are you Ipswich

Are you Ipswich

Are you Ipswich in disguise

Are you Ipswich in disguise

Your sister is your mother

Your father is your brother

Your f*ckin one another

The Ipswich family

The Best Norwich City Football Chants Ever ...

Your ground's too big for you
Your ground's too big for you
Your ground's too big for you

Build a bonfire

Build a bonfire

Put Ipswich on the top

Put Wolves in the middle

And we'll burn the f*cking lot

They're here
They're there
They're every f*cking where
Empty seats, empty seats

Stamford Bridge is falling down

Falling down, falling down

Stamford Bridge is falling down

Poor old Chelsea

The Best Norwich City Football Chants Ever ...

F*ck all
You've never won f*ck all
You've never won f*ck all
You've never won f*ck all

F*ck all
You've never won f*ck all

Jingle bells
Jingle bells
Jingle all the way
Oh what fun it is to see Norwich win away
Hey!
(Tune: Jingle Bells)

Who, Who, Who, Who ...
(Sung when the other team makes a substitution and the players name is announced)

The Best Norwich City Football Chants Ever ...

Stand up if you hate Ipswich
Stand up if you hate Ipswich
Stand up if you hate Ipswich

Sit down if you hate Ipswich
Sit down if you hate Ipswich
Sit down if you hate Ipswich

Dance round if you hate Ipswich
Dance round if you hate Ipswich
Dance round if you hate Ipswich

Dream on, Dream on
With envy in your heart
And you'll never with the league
You'll never win the league - again, again, again

You are a scouser, an ugly scouser
You're only happy on giro day
Your mum's out thieving
Your dad's drug dealing
But please don't take my hubcaps away

The Best Norwich City Football Chants Ever ...

Steve Gerrard, Gerrard
He kisses the badge on his chest
Then puts in a transfer request
Steve Gerrard, Gerrard

You scouse b***ards
You scouse b***ards
You scouse b***ards

Are you watching?
Are you watching?
Are you watching Ipswich
Are you watching Ipswich

If you hate Wolves clap your hands
If you hate Wolves clap your hands
If you hate Wolves
If you hate Wolves
If you hate Wolves
Clap your hands

Glory Hunters Man United!
Glory Hunters Man Untied!
Glory Hunters Man United!
Support Your Local Team!

Feed the scousers
Let them know it's Christmas time

My garden shed
(My garden shed)
Is bigger than this
(Is bigger than this)
My garden shed is bigger than this
It's got a door, and a window
My garden shed is bigger this

The Best Norwich City Football Chants Ever ...

If I had the wings of a sparrow
If I had the ar*e of a crow
I'd fly over Ipswich tomorrow
And sh*t on the b*stards below (below)
Sh*t on,,sh*t on
oh sh*t on the b*stards below

Chapter 4

*The referees a w*nker*

The Best Norwich City Football Chants Ever …

Chapter 4 - *The referees a w*nker*

The referees a w*nker
The referees a w*nker
The referees a w*nker

Where's your Father?
Where's your Father?
Where's your Father, referee
you ain't got one
your a B*stard
your a B*stard referee

12 men …
You've only got 12 men …
You've only got 12 men …

12 men …
You've only got 12 men …
You've only got 12 men …

The Best Norwich City Football Chants Ever ...

Chapter 5

The Best Norwich City Websites

The Best Norwich City Football Chants Ever ...

Chapter 5 - The Best Norwich City Websites

Official Web Site

www.canaries.co.uk

Unofficial Web Sites

www.norwich.vitalfootball.co.uk

www.norwichcity.footballunited.com

www.norwichcity.myfootballwriter.com

www.freewebs.com/barclayendchoir/

www.ex-canaries.co.uk

www.yarmy.co.uk

The Best Norwich City Football Chants Ever …

www.fitc.org.uk

www.inthehandsofthefans.co.uk

www.german-canaries.de

www.wrathofthebarclay.co.uk

www.forces2canaries.co.uk

www.norwichcity-mad.co.uk

www.ncfc-fans.co.uk

www.yellowarmy.co.uk

www.stellacanaries.com

www.capitalcanaries.com

The Best Norwich City Football Chants Ever …

www.yarmouthyellows.co.uk

www.kickitoff.co.uk

www.ncisa.co.uk

The Best Norwich City Football Chants Ever ...

Chapter 6

Norwich City Supporters Clubs

The Best Norwich City Football Chants Ever …

Chapter 6 - Norwich City Supporters Clubs

www.nycanaries.com

www.scancanaries.com

www.myspace.com/hampshirecanaries

www.inthehandsofthefans.co.uk

www.german-canaries.de

www.capitalcanaries.com

www.yarmouthyellows.co.uk

www.ncisa.co.uk

www.foncy.co.uk

The Best Norwich City Football Chants Ever …

Chapter 7

The Best of The Rest

The Best Norwich City Football Chants Ever ...

Chapter 7 - The Best of the Rest

Some of the best ever football chants from other teams.

"You're just a poor man's Evian, you're just a poor man's Evian"
Sung in the lower leagues to Buxton FC

"You're just a fat Eddie Murphy"
Sung about Jimmy Floyd Hasselbaink

You're not yodelling, You're not yodelling any more"
Sung when playing in Europe when playing any Swiss team

"We hate Tuesday, hate Tuesday"
Sung in response to Sheffield United's chant of "We hate Wednesday"

"You should've stayed on the telly"
Sung to Shearer during his brief reign as manager of Newcastle

The Best Norwich City Football Chants Ever ...

"Sit down Pinocchio, sit down Pinocchio"
Sung to Liverpool's Phil Thompson

"You've got Di Canio, we've got your stereo"
Liverpool fans in response to West Ham's chant of "We've got Di Canio"

"Two Andy Gorams, there's only two Andy Gorams"
Celtic fans to Andy Goram after it was revealed the keeper was diagnosed with schizophrenia

"It's just like watching The Bill"
Sung when police come onto the pitch to the tune of "it's just like watching Brazil"

The Best Norwich City Football Chants Ever ...

"Nani are you OK? Are you OK Nani"
Manchester United fans towards Michael Jackson look a like Nani to the tune of smooth criminal

The Best Norwich City Football Chants Ever ...

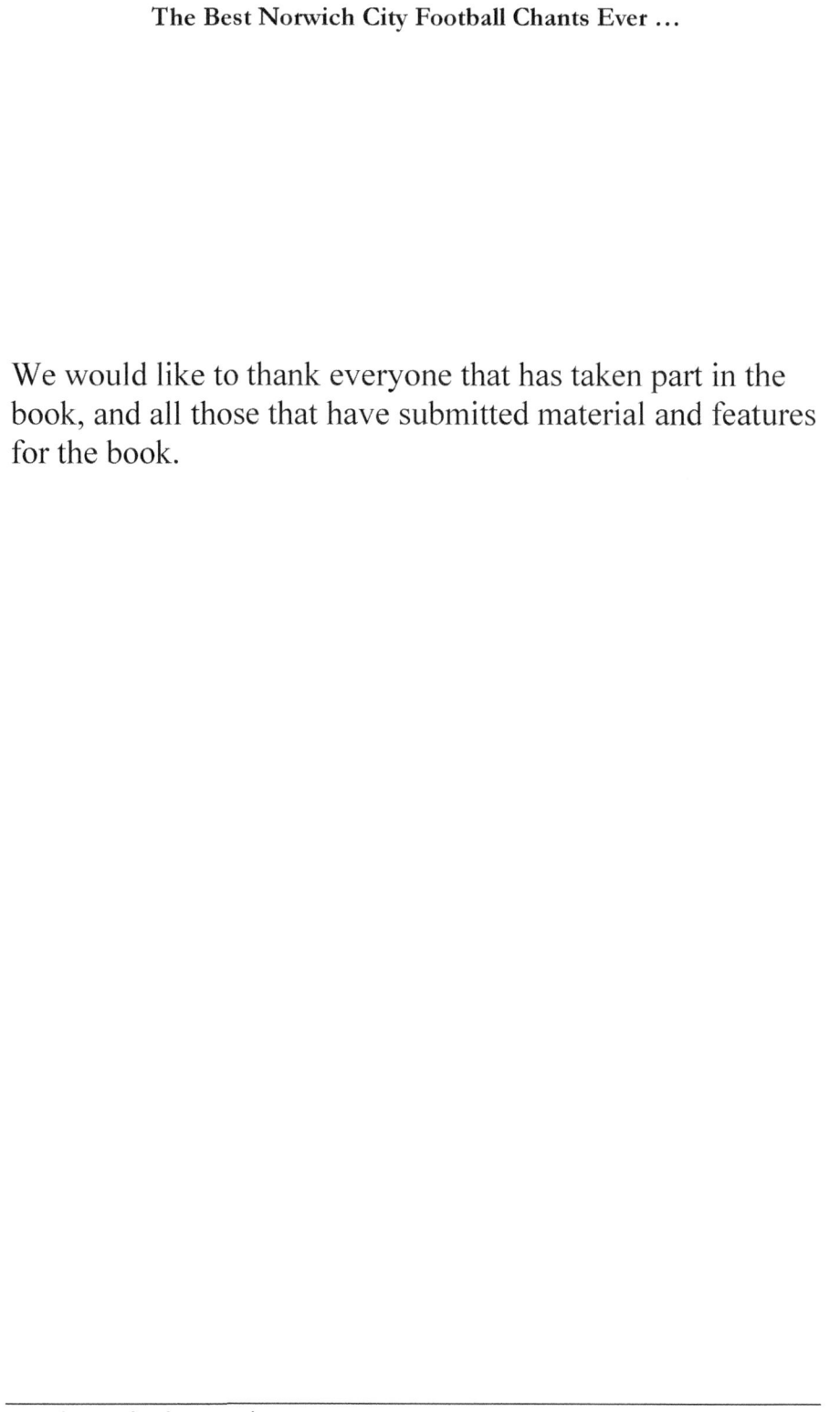

We would like to thank everyone that has taken part in the book, and all those that have submitted material and features for the book.

The Best Norwich City Football Chants Ever ...

The Best Norwich City Football Chants Ever ...

The Best Norwich City Football Chants Ever ...

Printed in Great Britain
by Amazon